Python Exercises with Data Structures and Algorithms

ISBN: 9798326448439

Copyright © 2024 by Haris Tsetsekas

Table of Contents

1. University Courses 5
2. Restaurant Reservations 9
3. Library 13
4. Contact List 19
5. Priority Todo List 23
6. Songs List 27
7. Task allocation 31
8. Word Frequencies 35
9. Syntax Checker 37
10. Maze Solver 41
11. File Indexer 47
12. Inventory with AVL Tree 51
13. Social Network 57
14. Flights 61
15. MNIST Image Comparison 65
16. HTTP Server with Caching 71
17. Distributed Auction 77

1. University Courses

Let's create a program that will handle the enrollment for university courses. Each course has one or more prerequisites, i.e. courses that must have been completed by a student in order to be able to enroll in the specific one.

Proposed Solution

First of all, we will define the class for a student in the university:

```
class Student:
    def __init__(self, id, name, course_count, courses):
        self.id = id
        self.name = name
        self.course_count = course_count
        self.courses = courses
```

Listing 1-1: university_courses.py

This class contains information about the student and the courses that have been completed successfully. The courses list contains the ID of the course.

Next, we define a class for the university courses:

```
class Course:
    def __init__(self, id, name, prereq_count, prereq_ids):
        self.id = id
        self.name = name
        self.prereq_count = prereq_count
        self.prereq_ids = prereq_ids

    #Check if the student can enroll in the course
    def can_enroll(self, student):
        for prereq_id in self.prereq_ids:
            has_prereq = False
            for course_id in student.courses:
                if course_id == prereq_id:
                    has_prereq = True
                    break
            if not has_prereq:
                return False
        return True
```

Listing 1-2: university_courses.py

Each course contains a list of the IDs of the prerequisite courses. The class also includes a method that finds out whether a student can enroll at a course. For each prerequisite course, this method tries to match it with a course already taken by the student.

Finally, the main() method:

```
def main():
    #Initialize the list of courses
```

```python
    courses = [
        Course(0, "Intro to Programming", 0, [-1]),
        Course(1, "Data Structures", 1, [0]),
        Course(2, "Algorithms", 1, [1]),
        Course(3, "Database Management", 1, [0]),
        Course(4, "Web Development", 1, [0]),
        Course(5, "Operating Systems", 2, [1, 2]),
        Course(6, "Computer Networks", 2, [1, 5]),
        Course(7, "Software Engineering", 2, [1, 2]),
        Course(8, "Machine Learning", 2, [1, 2]),
        Course(9, "Distributed Systems", 1, [5]),
        Course(10, "Cybersecurity", 2, [2, 3]),
        Course(11, "Cloud Computing", 2, [2, 3]),
        Course(12, "Mobile App Development", 1, [4]),
        Course(13, "Game Development", 1, [0]),
        Course(14, "Artificial Intelligence", 2, [2, 8]),
        Course(15, "Big Data Analytics", 2, [2, 3]),
        Course(16, "Blockchain Technology", 2, [2, 3]),
        Course(17, "UI/UX Design", 1, [14]),
        Course(18, "Embedded Systems", 2, [1, 5]),
        Course(19, "Computer Graphics", 1, [0])
    ]

    #Initialize a student
    student = Student(1, "John Doe", 5, [0, 1, 2, 3, 4])

    #Define the target courses the student wants to enroll in
    target_courses = [
        courses[13],   # Game Development
        courses[16],   # Blockchain Technology
        courses[17],   # UI/UX Design (student cannot enroll)
        courses[18]    # Embedded Systems
    ]

    #Print the enrollment status for each target course
    print("Enrollment status for " + student.name + ": ")
    for i in range(4):
        if target_courses[i].can_enroll(student):
            print("- Can enroll in " + target_courses[i].name)
        else:
            print("- Cannot enroll in " + target_courses[i].name
                + " due to missing prerequisites.")

if __name__ == "__main__":
    main()
```

Listing 1-3: university_courses.py

We create sample courses and a sample user that is still at the earlier stages of studies. We then try to find out if this student can enroll at 4 specific courses. We will see that the student will not be able to enroll at the most advanced ones, for lack of successfully completed prerequisite courses.

You can find this project in GitHub:

https://github.com/htset/python_exercises_dsa/tree/master/UniversityCourses

2. Restaurant Reservations

For this exercise, we will create a small program that will create table reservations for a restaurant. Each table is characterized by its capacity. For simplicity, we will split the reservation time in one-hour slots; a reservation can span multiple consecutive slots.

Proposed Solution

First of all, we will define the class for a customer:

```python
class Customer:
    def __init__(self, name: str):
        self.name = name
```

Listing 2-1: restaurant.py

This class contains the name of the customer. It could also include the customer phone number or other details.

Next, we define a class for the restaurant tables:

```python
class Table:
    def __init__(self, id: int, capacity: int):
        self.id = id
        self.capacity = capacity
```

Listing 2-2: restaurant.py

Each table object contains its ID as well as information about its capacity (the number of people it can accommodate).

Next, we define the Reservation class:

```python
class Reservation:
    def __init__(self, customer: Customer, table: Table, start_time_slot: int,
                 end_time_slot: int):
        self.customer = customer
        self.table = table
        self.start_time_slot = start_time_slot
        self.end_time_slot = end_time_slot
```

Listing 2-3: restaurant.py

Each reservation contains references to Customer and Table objects. It also contains the starting and the ending time slot (not inclusive).

We also create a Restaurant class that will implement the functionality for the creation of new reservations:

```python
class Restaurant:
    def __init__(self):
        self.tables = []         #List of tables in the restaurant
        self.reservations = []   #List of reservations
```

```python
def add_table(self, table: Table):
    self.tables.append(table)

...
```
Listing 2-4: restaurant.py

Method `add_table()` adds the reference of a table into the `tables` list.

In method `is_table_available()` we run a loop in the `reservations` list to determine if there exists a table that is not reserved in the specified timeslot.

```python
def is_table_available(self, table: Table, start_time_slot: int,
                       end_time_slot: int):
    #Check if the table is available for the given time slot
    for reservation in self.reservations:
        if reservation.table.id == table.id and (
            (start_time_slot >= reservation.start_time_slot
              and start_time_slot < reservation.end_time_slot) or
            (end_time_slot > reservation.start_time_slot
              and end_time_slot <= reservation.end_time_slot) or
            (start_time_slot <= reservation.start_time_slot
              and end_time_slot >= reservation.end_time_slot)
        ):
            return False
    return True
```
Listing 2-5: restaurant.py

Method `find_available_tables()` searches the `tables` list, in order to find all the tables that are available inside the specified timeslot (and have the required capacity).

```python
def find_available_tables(self, capacity: int, start_time_slot: int,
                          end_time_slot: int) :
    #Find tables that are available and have the required capacity
    available_tables = [
        table for table in self.tables
        if table.capacity >= capacity
        and self.is_table_available(table, start_time_slot, end_time_slot)
    ]
    #Sort available tables by capacity
    available_tables.sort(key=lambda table: table.capacity)
    return available_tables
```
Listing 2-6: restaurant.py

We filter the list of all tables to find those that have a capacity greater than or equal to the required capacity and are available during the specified time slot. This is done using a *list comprehension* that iterates over all tables and applies the `is_table_available()` method to check each table's availability.

After filtering the tables, we sort the list of available tables by their capacity in ascending order. This ensures that we prioritize smaller tables that fit the required capacity, which can help optimize the usage of larger tables for larger groups.

Next, the `add_reservation()` method will create a new reservation on the fly and will insert it into the `reservations` list. That's of course, if a suitable table is found. Note that we get the first table in the sorted list, i.e. the table with the smallest capacity.

```python
def add_reservation(self, name: str, capacity: int, start_slot: int,
                  end_slot: int):
    #Try to find available tables for the given capacity and time slot
    available_tables = self.find_available_tables(capacity, start_slot, end_slot)
    if available_tables:
        #If available, add a new reservation
        self.reservations.append(Reservation(
            Customer(name), available_tables[0], start_slot, end_slot))
        print("Reservation successfully added.")
    else:
        print("No available tables for the requested time slot.")
```

Listing 2-7: restaurant.py

Next, we have a method to print all the reservations in the console:

```python
def print_reservations(self):
    print("All reservations:")
    for reservation in self.reservations:
        print(f"Customer: {reservation.customer.name}, "
            f"Table Capacity: {reservation.table.capacity}, "
            f"Start Time Slot: {reservation.start_time_slot}, "
            f"End Time Slot: {reservation.end_time_slot}")
```

Listing 2-8: restaurant.py

Finally, in the `main()` method, we add tables to the `Restaurant` object and try to make reservations for specific capacities and timeslots. Some will be successful, but for others there will not be any table available. At the end, we print all the available reservations in the system.

```python
def main():
    restaurant = Restaurant()

    #Add tables to the restaurant
    restaurant.add_table(Table(1, 6))
    restaurant.add_table(Table(2, 4))
    restaurant.add_table(Table(3, 2))

    #Try to add reservations
    restaurant.add_reservation("Customer 1", 4, 1, 3)
    restaurant.add_reservation("Customer 2", 6, 2, 4)
    restaurant.add_reservation("Customer 3", 4, 3, 5)
    restaurant.add_reservation("Customer 4", 4, 1, 3)
```

```
    #Print all reservations
    restaurant.print_reservations()

if __name__ == "__main__":
    main()
```

Listing 2-9: restaurant.py

You can find this project in GitHub:

https://github.com/htset/python_exercises_dsa/tree/master/Restaurant

3. Library

Here we will create a console application for a library. Users will be able to enter books and list all the titles available in the library. They will also be able to lend books, return books as well as list all the book lending events. The books and the lending events will be stored in text files.

Proposed Solution

Let's begin with the definition of the Book and LendingEvent classes:

```
class Book:
    def __init__(self, title: str, author: str, available: int):
        self.title = title
        self.author = author
        self.available = available
```

Listing 3-1: book.py

```
from datetime import datetime

class LendingEvent:
    def __init__(self, book_title: str, user_name: str,
                 lending_date: datetime, returned: int):
        self.book_title = book_title
        self.user_name = user_name
        self.lending_date = lending_date
        self.returned = returned
```

Listing 3-2: lending_event.py

For each book, we record the title and the author. We also keep information about whether it is available or is currently lent (1 or 0 respectively).

For each lending event we record the book title and the name of the library user that has borrowed it. We also keep the lending date as well as an integer value of whether it has been returned or not (1 or 0 respectively).

We also define the Library class, that contains all the functionality for adding and displaying book information:

```
from datetime import datetime
import os

from book import Book
from lending_event import LendingEvent

class Library:
    BooksFilename = "books.txt"
    LendingFilename = "lending_events.txt"

    ...
```

Listing 3-3: library.py

The first method of class Library is used to add a new book in library catalog:

```python
def add_book(self):
    #Prompt user for book details
    title = input("Book title: ")
    author = input("Author: ")

    #Mark book as available
    book = Book(title, author, 1)

    #Append book details to books file
    with open(self.BooksFilename, 'a') as file:
        file.write(f"{book.title}|{book.author}|{book.available}\n")

    print("Book added successfully.")
```

Listing 3-4: library.py

After we get the book title and author from the user, we create a new Book object, Then, we open the books file with open(). The second parameter to the function is 'a', which means that we will append to the end of the file and the current contents will not be erased. Finally, we write the contents of the new book object at the end of the file. The following format is used:

book title|book author|Available (0 or 1)

Next, we implement the listing of the books:

```python
def list_books(self):
    #Check if books file exists
    if not os.path.exists(self.BooksFilename):
        print("No books entered so far")
        return

    print("Books available in the library:")
    with open(self.BooksFilename, 'r') as file:
        for line in file:
            parts = line.strip().split('|')
            print(f"Title: {parts[0]}")
            print(f"Author: {parts[1]}")
            print(f"Available: {'True' if parts[2] == '1' else 'False'}")
            print("------------------------------")
```

Listing 3-5: library.py

Here, we open the file from the beginning, and we use a loop to read the details of each book from the text file.

We proceed with the book lending functionality:

```python
    def lend_book(self):
        #Check if books file exists
        if not os.path.exists(self.BooksFilename):
            print("No books entered so far")
            return

        book_title = input("Enter the title of the book to lend: ")

        #Read all lines from books file
        with open(self.BooksFilename, 'r') as file:
            lines = file.readlines()

        book_found = False

        #Search for the book in the list
        for i in range(len(lines)):
            parts = lines[i].strip().split('|')
            if parts[0] == book_title and parts[2] == '1':
                lines[i] = f"{parts[0]}|{parts[1]}|0\n"
                book_found = True

                user_name = input("Enter your name: ")

                #Write lending event to lending file
                with open(self.LendingFilename, 'a') as lending_file:
                    lending_file.write(
                        f"{book_title}|{user_name}|{datetime.now()}|0\n")

                print(f"Book '{book_title}' has been lent to {user_name}.")
                break

        if not book_found:
            print(f"Book '{book_title}' not found or not available.")

        #Write updated book details back to books file
        with open(self.BooksFilename, 'w') as file:
            file.writelines(lines)
```

Listing 3-6: library.py

We first try to find the requested book by reading all the entries from the books file in a list of strings.

We iterate this list and we split each entry into the book details (title, author, availability). When we find the book and (if it is available), we mark it as not currently available.

Afterwards, we record the lending event by writing a new entry at the end of the respective file. Finally, we write all the entries in the books list back to the books text file, overwriting the file.

Next, we present the functionality for returning a book:

```python
    def return_book(self):
        if not os.path.exists(self.LendingFilename):
            print("No lending events entered so far")
            return

        book_title = input("Enter the title of the book to return: ")

        #Read all lines from books file
        with open(self.BooksFilename, 'r') as file:
            books_lines = file.readlines()

        book_found = False

        #Search for the book in the list
        for i in range(len(books_lines)):
            parts = books_lines[i].strip().split('|')
            if parts[0] == book_title and parts[2] == '0':
                books_lines[i] = f"{parts[0]}|{parts[1]}|1\n"
                book_found = True

                #Read all lines from lending file
                with open(self.LendingFilename, 'r') as lending_file:
                    lending_lines = lending_file.readlines()

                #Search for the lending event
                for j in range(len(lending_lines)):
                    lending_parts = lending_lines[j].strip().split('|')
                    if lending_parts[0] == book_title and lending_parts[3] == '0':
                        lending_lines[j] = (
                            f"{lending_parts[0]}|{lending_parts[1]}|"
                            f"{lending_parts[2]}|1\n"
                        )
                        print(f"Book '{book_title}' has been returned.")
                        break

                #Write updated lending events back to lending file
                with open(self.LendingFilename, 'w') as lending_file:
                    lending_file.writelines(lending_lines)
                break

        if not book_found:
            print(f"Book '{book_title}' not found or already returned.")

        #Write updated book details back to books file
        with open(self.BooksFilename, 'w') as file:
            file.writelines(books_lines)
```

Listing 3-7: library.py

Here, we read again all the book file entries into a list of strings, and we try to find the requested file. Then, we read all the book lending events from the respective file and we search for the lending event of the specific book.

If we find the event, then we change its status to "returned" and we write all the entries back to the lending file. Finally, we also store all the book entries into the respective file, after having updated the book availability status back to 1 again.

Now, let's see the events listing method:

```python
    def list_lending_events(self):
        if not os.path.exists(self.LendingFilename):
            print("No lending events entered so far")
            return

        print("Lending events:")
        with open(self.LendingFilename, 'r') as file:
            for line in file:
                parts = line.strip().split('|')
                print(f"Book Title: {parts[0]}")
                print(f"User Name: {parts[1]}")
                print(f"Lending Date: {parts[2]}")
                print(f"Returned: {'True' if parts[3] == '1' else 'False'}")
                print("------------------------------")
```

Listing 3-8: library.py

And finally, the `main()` function that handles the interaction with the user:

```python
import sys
from library import Library

def main():
    lib = Library()
    while True:
        print("\n1. Add a book\n2. List all books\n3. Lend a book"
              "\n4. Return a book\n5. List lending events\n0. Exit")
        choice = input("Enter your choice: ")

        try:
            choice = int(choice)
        except ValueError:
            print("Invalid choice. Please enter a number.")
            continue

        if choice == 1:
            lib.add_book()
        elif choice == 2:
            lib.list_books()
        elif choice == 3:
            lib.lend_book()
        elif choice == 4:
            lib.return_book()
        elif choice == 5:
            lib.list_lending_events()
        elif choice == 0:
            print("Exiting.")
            sys.exit()
```

```
        else:
            print("Invalid choice. Please try again.")

if __name__ == "__main__":
    main()
```
Listing 3-9: library.py

You can find this project in GitHub:

https://github.com/htset/python_exercises_dsa/tree/master/Library

4. Contact List

In this exercise, we will create a list that will store the names and the phone numbers of our contacts. For faster search performance, the contacts will be stored in a *hash map* structure.

Proposed Solution

A *hash map*, also known as a *hash table*, is a data structure that efficiently organizes and retrieves data based on key-value pairs. It employs a technique called *hashing*, where each key is mapped to a unique index in a list using a hash function. This mapping allows for rapid insertion, deletion, and retrieval of values based on their associated keys.

In cases where multiple keys hash to the same index (known as *collisions*), hash maps often employ strategies such as *chaining* to handle these collisions gracefully and maintain performance.

Here is the definition of the classes used:

```python
class Contact:
    def __init__(self):
        self.name = None
        self.phone = None
        self.next = None

class ContactList:
    HASH_SIZE = 100

    def __init__(self):
        self.bucket_table = [None] * self.HASH_SIZE

    ...
```

Listing 4-1: contact_list.py

The ContactList class contains a table of 100 entries. Each entry contains a reference to a Contact object. The Contact class contains the name and the phone number, as well as a reference to another Contact object, making it a linked list node. Essentially, the ContactList class is a list of linked lists; in this way the contact list can expand as we add new elements, avoiding collisions.

A contact will be inserted into one of the buckets according to its specific hash number. We will use a hash function that will create a number between 0 and 99 based on the contact's name string:

```python
    def hash(self, name):
        hash_value = 5381
        for char in name:
            hash_value = ((hash_value << 5) + hash_value) + ord(char)
        return abs(hash_value) % self.HASH_SIZE
```

Listing 4-2: contact_list.py

This method is based on a hash function written by Daniel J. Bernstein (also know as *djb*)[1]. This method returns the index of the hash map, where we should insert the specific contact.

Here is the code for the contact addition:

```python
def contact_add(self, name, phone):
    #get index from contact name
    hash_index = self.hash(name)
    new_contact = Contact()
    new_contact.name = name
    new_contact.phone = phone
    new_contact.next = self.bucket_table[hash_index]
    self.bucket_table[hash_index] = new_contact
```

Listing 4-3: contact_list.py

We first calculate the hash index based on the contact's name and then we create a new `Contact` object. After populating the object properties, we insert the object at the beginning of the respective bucket.

Here is the code for contact removal:

```python
def contact_remove(self, name):
    index = self.hash(name)
    contact = self.bucket_table[index]
    previous = None

    while contact is not None:
        if contact.name == name:
            if previous is None:
                #Contact to remove is the head of the list
                self.bucket_table[index] = contact.next
            else:
                #Contact to remove is not the head of the list
                previous.next = contact.next
            print(f"Contact '{name}' removed successfully.")
            return
        previous = contact
        contact = contact.next
    print(f"Contact '{name}' not found.")
```

Listing 4-4: contact_list.py

To remove an entry, we first need to get its hash value. We use this integer value as the index to get the respective bucket. We then search the bucket entries, one by one, until we locate the specific contact. We then remove the entry from the buckets, in the same way we remove a node from a linked list.

Next, the code for contact search is presented:

---

[1] http://www.cse.yorku.ca/~oz/hash.html

```python
    def contact_search(self, name):
        hash_index = self.hash(name)
        contact = self.bucket_table[hash_index]
        while contact is not None:
            if contact.name == name:
                print(f"Name: {contact.name}\nPhone Number: {contact.phone}")
                return
            contact = contact.next
        print(f"Contact '{name}' not found.")
```

Listing 4-5: contact_list.py

Finally, in the main code, we create a phonebook and we use it to add, remove and search contacts:

```python
if __name__ == "__main__":
    phonebook = ContactList()
    phonebook.contact_add("John", "235454545")
    phonebook.contact_add("Jane", "775755454")
    phonebook.contact_add("George", "4344343477")

    phonebook.contact_search("John")
    phonebook.contact_search("Alex")
    phonebook.contact_search("George")

    phonebook.contact_remove("Jake")
    phonebook.contact_remove("Jane")
    phonebook.contact_search("Jane")
```

Listing 4-6: contact_list.py

You can find this project in GitHub:

https://github.com/htset/python_exercises_dsa/tree/master/ContactList

5. Priority Todo List

We are going to implement a simple todo list application. Each entry will contain the task description as well as a number that will signify its priority (top priority is equal to 1).

The todo list will be implemented using a *linked list*. Apart from the options to add, delete and display tasks, there will also be functionality to sort the linked list using *bubble sort*.

Proposed Solution

First let's see the main function, in *todo.py*:

```python
from todo_list import TodoList

if __name__ == "__main__":
    todo_list = TodoList()

    while True:
        print("\nTo-Do List Manager")
        print("1. Add Task")
        print("2. Remove Task")
        print("3. Display Tasks")
        print("4. Sort Tasks by Priority")
        print("0. Exit")
        choice = input("Enter your choice: ")

        try:
            choice = int(choice)
            if choice == 1:
                description = input("Enter task description: ")
                priority = int(input("Enter priority: "))
                todo_list.add_task(description, priority)
                print("Task added successfully.")
            elif choice == 2:
                index = int(input("Enter number of task to remove: "))
                todo_list.remove_task(index - 1)
                print("Task removed successfully.")
            elif choice == 3:
                print("List of tasks:")
                todo_list.display_tasks()
            elif choice == 4:
                todo_list.sort_tasks()
                print("Tasks sorted by priority.")
            elif choice == 0:
                print("Exiting...")
                break
            else:
                print("Invalid choice. Please try again.")
        except ValueError:
            print("Invalid input. Please enter a number.")
```

Listing 5-1: todo.py

The main function handles the user input and calls the respective methods of the `TodoList` object.

Here is the definition of the Task class that makes the objects of the linked list structure:

```python
class Task:
    def __init__(self, description=None, priority=0):
        self.description = description
        self.priority = priority
        self.next = None
```

Listing 5-2: task.py

The linked list consists of `Task` nodes that get linked one to the other via the `next` reference. The `head` variable points to the first element in the list:

```python
from task import Task

class TodoList:
    def __init__(self):
        self.head = None
        self.size = 0

    ...
```

Listing 5-3: todo_list.py

The class constructor initializes the linked list structure.

The `add_task()` method creates a new task node and inserts it at the end of the linked list:

```python
    def add_task(self, description, priority):
        task = Task(description, priority)
        if self.head is None:
            #List is empty
            self.head = task
        else:
            temp = self.head
            #Find the last node
            while temp.next is not None:
                temp = temp.next
            #Insert the new task after the last node
            temp.next = task
        self.size += 1
```

Listing 5-4: todo_list.py

Next, we define the `remove_task()` method:

```python
    def remove_task(self, index):
        if self.head is None:
            print("List is empty.")
            return
```

```python
        if index == 0:
            #If we remove the first item in the list
            temp = self.head
            self.head = self.head.next
            temp = None
            self.size -= 1
            return

        previous = None
        current = self.head
        i = 0
        #Go to the selected index
        while current is not None and i < index:
            previous = current
            current = current.next
            i += 1

        if current is None:
            print("Index out of bounds.")
            return

        previous.next = current.next
        current = None
        self.size -= 1
```
Listing 5-5: todo_list.py

The argument to the method is the index of the entry inside the linked list, as it is presented during task listing in the console. As we will see in the next snippet, we start listing the tasks from number 1, which is something that we take into account in the calculations above.

Here is the code for the task listing:

```python
    def display_tasks(self):
        temp = self.head
        i = 1
        while temp is not None:
            print(f"{i}) Description: {temp.description}, Priority: {temp.priority}")
            temp = temp.next
            i += 1
```
Listing 5-6: todo_list.py

Finally, we present the code for the sorting of tasks according to their priority:

```python
    def sort_tasks(self):
        if self.head is None:
            return

        swapped = True
        while swapped:
            swapped = False
            ptr1 = self.head
```

```
        while ptr1.next is not None:
            if ptr1.priority > ptr1.next.priority:
                #Swap data of adjacent nodes
                ptr1.priority, ptr1.next.priority = \
                    ptr1.next.priority, ptr1.priority
                ptr1.description, ptr1.next.description = \
                    ptr1.next.description, ptr1.description
                swapped = True
            ptr1 = ptr1.next
```

Listing 5-7: todo_list.py

The code employs the *bubble sort* algorithm to perform the task sorting operation. In bubble sort, we perform multiple passes of the linked list. Each time we find a task that has lower priority than its next task, then we perform swapping of those adjacent tasks. Note how we perform swapping in one line.

Over time, all entries will be sorted according to priority and there will eventually be a loop pass where no swapping will occur. This is when the algorithm will end.

You can find this project in GitHub:

https://github.com/htset/python_exercises_dsa/tree/master/Todo

6. Songs List

Let's create a simple program that takes a list of songs and sorts them by artist, album or release date, using *insertion sort*.

Proposed Solution

The Song class will contain information about the title of the song, the artist, the album and the release year:

```python
class Song:
    def __init__(self, title, artist, album, release_year):
        self.title = title
        self.artist = artist
        self.album = album
        self.release_year = release_year
```

Listing 6-1: songs.py

Next, we define three functions, that will be used for the comparisons:

```python
#Compare songs based on artist
def compare_by_artist(a, b):
    return (a.artist > b.artist) - (a.artist < b.artist)

#Compare songs based on album
def compare_by_album(a, b):
    return (a.album > b.album) - (a.album < b.album)

#Compare songs based on release date
def compare_by_release_date(a, b):
    return a.release_year - b.release_year
```

Listing 6-2: songs.py

In the first two functions, we compare two strings, while in the third one we compare two integers. The compare_by_* functions return -1, 0, or 1 based on the comparison, which is suitable for Python's sort functions.

Those functions will be used by the insertion_sort() function:

```python
def insertion_sort(arr, comparator):
    for i in range(1, len(arr)):
        key = arr[i]
        j = i - 1
        #Move elements of arr[0..i-1], that are greater than key,
        # to one position ahead of their current position
        while j >= 0 and comparator(arr[j], key) > 0:
            arr[j + 1] = arr[j]
            j -= 1
        arr[j + 1] = key
```

Listing 6-3: songs.py

We pass a function reference (`comparator`) as argument to the `insertion_sort()` function to specify the comparison logic for sorting the songs list.

For instance, if we call `insertion_sort()` like this:

```
insertion_sort(songs, compare_by_artist)
```

then, the following code inside `insertion_sort()`:

```
while j >= 0 and comparator(arr[j], key) > 0:
```

will result in calling the `compare_by_artist()` function. In this way, we don't have to write `insertion_sort()` three times to accommodate for the three different types of comparison.

Insertion sort works by taking each element in the list and moving it to the left part of the list in a sorted position. At any time, the left part of the list is sorted, while we take items from the right part. As we move an element to a place in the list, all the items to the right will have to move one place to the right.

This is all illustrated in the `main()` function, where we call `insertion_sort()` three times, each time passing a different comparison function. Each time, the list is sorted in a different way:

```python
def main():
    songs = [
        Song("Song1", "Artist2", "Album1", 2010),
        Song("Song2", "Artist1", "Album2", 2005),
        Song("Song3", "Artist3", "Album1", 2015),
        Song("Song4", "Artist4", "Album3", 2008),
        Song("Song5", "Artist1", "Album2", 2003),
        Song("Song6", "Artist3", "Album4", 2019),
        Song("Song7", "Artist2", "Album3", 2012),
        Song("Song8", "Artist4", "Album4", 2017),
        Song("Song9", "Artist5", "Album5", 2014),
        Song("Song10", "Artist5", "Album5", 2011)
    ]

    #Sort by artist
    insertion_sort(songs, compare_by_artist)
    print("Sorted by Artist:")
    for song in songs:
        print(f"{song.title} from {song.artist}")
    print()

    #Sort by album
    insertion_sort(songs, compare_by_album)
    print("Sorted by Album:")
    for song in songs:
        print(f"{song.title} from {song.album}")
    print()
```

```
    #Sort by release date
    insertion_sort(songs, compare_by_release_date)
    print("Sorted by Release Date:")
    for song in songs:
        print(f"{song.title} released in {song.release_year}")

if __name__ == "__main__":
    main()
```

Listing 6-4: songs.py

You can find this project in GitHub:

https://github.com/htset/python_exercises_dsa/tree/master/Songs

7. Task allocation

We will create a program where users can enter the description of tasks and their durations. The tasks will be allocated to workers, based on the amount of work that they already have taken over. This means that the task will be allocated to the worker with the lower workload.

Proposed Solution

We will use a *priority queue* to express the differences in priority between the various workers, based on their workload so far.

Let's first define the `Task` and `Worker` classes:

```python
import heapq  #for priority queue
from typing import List
import sys

class Task:
    def __init__(self, description: str, duration: int):
        self.description = description
        self.duration = duration
```

Listing 7-1: task_allocation.py

The `Task` class consists of the task description and duration in minutes.

```python
class Worker:
    def __init__(self, worker_id: int, workload: int):
        self.id = worker_id
        self.workload = workload

    def __lt__(self, other):
        #Used to compare (less-than <) Worker objects,
        return self.workload < other.workload
```

Listing 7-2: task_allocation.py

The `Worker` class contains the ID of the worker as well as the workload (also in minutes).

Next, we define the `main()` method:

```python
class TaskAllocation:
    def __init__(self):
        self.tasks = []
        self.worker_queue = []

    def main(self):
        num_workers = int(input("Enter the number of workers: "))

        #Initialize workers with ID and 0 workload
        for i in range(num_workers):
            heapq.heappush(self.worker_queue, Worker(i, 0))
```

```python
while True:
    print("\nMenu:")
    print("1. Add Task")
    print("2. Display Tasks")
    print("3. Print Workers Queue")
    print("4. Exit")
    choice = int(input("Enter your choice: "))

    if choice == 1:
        self.add_task()
    elif choice == 2:
        self.display_tasks()
    elif choice == 3:
        self.print_workers_queue()
    elif choice == 4:
        print("Exiting program...")
        break
    else:
        print("Invalid choice! Please try again.")

...
```
Listing 7-3: task_allocation.py

The `main()` method displays the menu and gets the user's selections. It also initializes a list that will store the tasks, and a priority queue that will contain the workers.

`heapq` is a module in Python that provides an implementation of the heap queue algorithm, also known as the priority queue algorithm. Note that `self.worker_queue` is a simple Python list. We use the `heapq` module to use it as a priority queue.

Also note that when the program starts, the users should select the total number of workers; the workers will be subsequently referred to by their ID.

Next, we implement the method that adds a new task to the system:

```python
#Method to add a task and allocate it to a worker
def add_task(self):
    description = input("Enter task description: ")
    duration = int(input("Enter task duration (in minutes): "))

    if len(self.worker_queue) == 0:
        print("No workers available! Task cannot be assigned.")
        return

    #Dequeue the worker with the shortest workload
    worker = heapq.heappop(self.worker_queue)

    #Assign the task to the worker and update workload
    self.tasks.append(Task(description, duration))
    print(f"Task added successfully and allocated to Worker {worker.id}!")
```

```
        #Update workload
        worker.workload += duration

        #Store updated worker back to queue
        heapq.heappush(self.worker_queue, worker)
```

Listing 7-4: task_allocation.py

In order to find the worker that has the lowest workload, we store workers in the priority queue. Note that we are using the workload property as the parameter that will be used to sort the priority queue. This is specified in the definition of the less-than (__lt__) method in the Worker class:

```
    def __lt__(self, other):
        #Used to compare (less-than <) Worker objects,
        return self.workload < other.workload
```

When we dequeue an item from the queue, then we will get the item with lowest workload.

In add_task(), we get the worker with the lowest workload (the one that is positioned at the front of the queue) and we add the task's workload to the worker's own workload. Then, we store the task into the tasks list. Finally, the worker is inserted into the queue again; now the worker will be positioned according to the newly updated workload.

Finally, we present the code for two other operations, displaying the tasks and the workers information respectively:

```
    #Method to display all tasks
    def display_tasks(self):
        print("Task List:")
        for task in self.tasks:
            print(f"Task description: {task.description}, "
                  "Duration: {task.duration} minutes")

    #Method to print the workers queue
    def print_workers_queue(self):
        print("Workers Queue:")
        #heapq does not support direct iteration, we need to copy the heap to display
        temp_queue = list(self.worker_queue)
        heapq.heapify(temp_queue)
        while temp_queue:
            worker = heapq.heappop(temp_queue)
            print(f"Worker ID: {worker.id}, Workload: {worker.workload} minutes")


if __name__ == "__main__":
    TaskAllocation().main()
```

Listing 7-5: task_allocation.py

Note that, the way we have written the `print_workers_queue()` method, we will get a copy of the *ordered* workers list. We could also directly iterate over the `self.worker_queue` list. Since Python's `heapq` maintains the heap invariant, iterating over the list will print the workers in the order they are stored in the heap, but it won't necessarily be in workload order unless we pop them from the heap.

You can find this project in GitHub:

https://github.com/htset/python_exercises_dsa/tree/master/TaskAllocation

8. Word Frequencies

We will create a simple program that will parse a text file and will find the frequencies of all the words that appear in it.

Proposed Solution

This project is a use case for a dictionary structure. We will use a `defaultdict` class that will store word and word frequency pairs. `defaultdict` is a subclass of Python's built-in `dict` class, part of the `collections` module. It provides a default value for the dictionary being accessed if the key is not already present. This can simplify the code by removing the need to check if a key is in the dictionary before setting or updating its value.

Here is the program code:

```python
from collections import defaultdict

def clean_word(word):
    #Remove non-letter characters and convert to lowercase
    return ''.join([char.lower() for char in word if char.isalpha()])

def main():
    word_frequency = defaultdict(int)  #Dictionary to store word frequencies

    #Read text from file
    try:
        with open('input.txt', 'r') as input_file:
            for line in input_file:
                #Split each line into words
                words = line.split()
                for word in words:
                    #Clean each word
                    cleaned_word = clean_word(word)
                    if cleaned_word:
                        #Update the word frequency
                        word_frequency[cleaned_word] += 1
    except IOError as e:
        print(e)   #Handle any IO exceptions

    #Display word frequencies
    print("Word Frequencies:")
    for word, frequency in word_frequency.items():
        print(f"{word}: {frequency}")

if __name__ == "__main__":
    main()
```

Listing 8-1: word_frequencies.py

Initially, we are reading the input file, line by line. Then, we split each line, based on spaces and we process each word to make it lowercase and remove non-letter characters. This processing is performed by the `clean_word()` method, that takes a string, breaks it into characters, then filters the characters to keep only letters and numbers. Finally, it maps each character into lowercase ones and creates a new string based on them.

Then, we add the word in the dictionary. If the word does not already exist in the `defaultdict`, then a new entry will be created with a default frequency of zero. Otherwise, the frequency for the existing entry will be incremented.

Finally, we employ a loop to print all the words and their frequencies to the console.

You can find this project in GitHub:

https://github.com/htset/python_exercises_dsa/tree/master/WordFrequencies

9. Syntax Checker

Let's create a trivial syntax checker that will scan a source code file and will determine whether the parentheses, brackets, or braces in the code are balanced or not.

Proposed Solution

In various languages, like C, C++, Java etc., when we open a series of parentheses, brackets, or braces, we have to make sure that they are closed in the reverse order.

The fact that items entered in a *stack* are extracted in the reverse order, makes it suitable for this algorithm:

```python
class Stack:
    def __init__(self):
        self.items = []  #Initialize an empty list to store stack items

    ...
```

Listing 9-1: syntax_checker.py

Next, we add the code for stack *push* and *pop*, as well as a method to check if the stack is empty:

```python
    def push(self, c):
        self.items.append(c)   #Append the character to the stack

    def pop(self):
        if self.is_empty():
            print("Stack is empty")
            exit(1)   #Exit if the stack is empty
        return self.items.pop()   #Pop and return the top item

    def is_empty(self):
        return len(self.items) == 0   #Return True if the stack is empty
```

Listing 9-2: syntax_checker.py

The most interesting part of the code is the algorithm that checks whether the file is balanced or not:

```python
class SyntaxChecker:
    @staticmethod
    def check_balanced(filename):
        try:
            with open(filename, 'r') as file:
                stack = Stack()

                while True:
                    #Read one character at a time
                    c = file.read(1)
                    if not c:  # End of file
                        break
```

```python
            if c in '([{':
                #If the character is an opening bracket
                stack.push(c)
            elif c in ')]}':
                #If the character is a closing bracket
                if stack.is_empty():
                    return 0

                opening_char = stack.pop()

                #Check if the closing bracket matches the opening bracket
                if (c == ')' and opening_char != '(') or \
                   (c == ']' and opening_char != '[') or \
                   (c == '}' and opening_char != '{'):
                    return 0

        #Return 1 if balanced, 0 otherwise
        return 1 if stack.is_empty() else 0
    except IOError as e:
        print(e)
        return 0

    @staticmethod
    def main():
        try:
            filename = input("Path to the source file: ")

            if SyntaxChecker.check_balanced(filename) == 1:
                print("The input file is balanced.")
            else:
                print("The input file is not balanced.")
        except IOError as e:
            print(e)


if __name__ == "__main__":
    SyntaxChecker.main()
```

Listing 9-3: syntax_checker.py

We open and parse the source code file, and we push the bracket *opening* characters into the stack. When we encounter a *closing* character, then we pop the first available opening character from the stack.

If there is a mismatch between those two characters, we conclude that the file is not balanced. At the end, we also check that the stack is emptied; if not, then the file is still unbalanced.

Note that this is a trivial version of the algorithm. There will be times that a source file that compiles will be found to be unbalanced. An example for this would be the following code (in Java) where we use single characters (opening or closing) in our code during checking:

```
if (c == '(' || c == '[' || c == '{')
```

A more advanced version of the algorithm would not take those characters (e.g. those enclosed in quotes) into account.

You can find this project in GitHub:

https://github.com/htset/python_exercises_dsa/tree/master/SyntaxChecker

10. Maze Solver

In this exercise, we will use a *stack* to find our way through a maze.

Proposed Solution

We will define a maze as a two-dimensional list of integers. The walls will be marked with ones (1), while the corridors of the maze will be marked with zeroes (0).

Below, we can see the definition of a 15x15 maze:

```
self.matrix = [
    [0, 1, 0, 0, 0, 0, 0, 0, 0, 0, 0, 0, 0, 0, 0],
    [0, 1, 0, 1, 0, 1, 1, 1, 1, 0, 1, 1, 1, 1, 0],
    [0, 1, 0, 1, 0, 1, 0, 0, 0, 0, 1, 0, 0, 0, 0],
    [0, 0, 0, 1, 0, 1, 0, 1, 1, 1, 1, 0, 1, 1, 0],
    [0, 1, 0, 1, 0, 1, 0, 0, 0, 0, 1, 0, 1, 0, 0],
    [0, 1, 0, 1, 0, 1, 1, 1, 1, 0, 1, 0, 1, 1, 0],
    [0, 1, 0, 1, 0, 0, 0, 0, 1, 0, 1, 0, 0, 0, 0],
    [0, 1, 0, 1, 1, 1, 1, 0, 1, 0, 1, 0, 1, 1, 0],
    [0, 1, 0, 0, 0, 0, 1, 0, 1, 0, 1, 0, 0, 1, 0],
    [0, 1, 1, 1, 1, 0, 1, 0, 1, 0, 1, 0, 1, 1, 0],
    [0, 0, 0, 0, 1, 0, 1, 0, 1, 0, 1, 0, 0, 0, 0],
    [0, 1, 1, 0, 1, 0, 1, 0, 1, 0, 1, 1, 1, 1, 0],
    [0, 0, 1, 0, 1, 0, 0, 0, 1, 0, 0, 0, 0, 1, 0],
    [0, 1, 1, 1, 1, 1, 1, 1, 1, 1, 1, 0, 1, 0],
    [0, 0, 0, 0, 0, 0, 0, 0, 0, 0, 0, 0, 0, 1, 0]
]
```

Listing 10-1: maze_solver.py

The entrance of the maze is at the top left corner, and the exit at the bottom right corner.

We will use a stack structure to solve this maze. As we move through the maze, we store the entered point coordinates in the stack. When we reach a dead end, then we will have to backtrack, and we will do this by popping one point from the stack. This algorithm is called *Depth-first search (DFS)*, as it goes inside the maze as deep as possible, only to go back and try another direction when no way is found.

Here is the code for the coordinate points:

```
class Point:
    def __init__(self, row=0, col=0):
        self.row = row
        self.col = col
```

Listing 10-2: maze_solver.py

And here is the code for the stack:

```
class Stack:
    def __init__(self, capacity):
        #Initialize stack with a fixed capacity
```

```python
        self.items = [None] * capacity
        #Initialize top index
        self.top = -1

    #Check if stack is empty
    def is_empty(self):
        return self.top == -1

    #Push item onto stack
    def push(self, item):
        self.top += 1
        self.items[self.top] = item

    #Return top item
    def pop(self):
        if self.is_empty():
            print("Stack is empty")
            exit(1)
        item = self.items[self.top]
        self.top -= 1
        return item
```

Listing 10-3: maze_solver.py

Note that we keep the stack simple and don't include bounds checking, as we will instantiate a stack with the maximum capacity needed to solve the maze (*ROWS*COLS*).

Now, it is time to introduce a class that will handle the maze:

```python
class Maze:
    ROWS = 15
    COLS = 15

    def __init__(self):
        #Create a stack with a size equal to total cells
        self.stack = Stack(self.ROWS * self.COLS)
        self.matrix = [
            [0, 1, 0, 0, 0, 0, 0, 0, 0, 0, 0, 0, 0, 0, 0],
            [0, 1, 0, 1, 0, 1, 1, 1, 1, 0, 1, 1, 1, 1, 0],
            [0, 1, 0, 1, 0, 1, 0, 0, 0, 0, 1, 0, 0, 0, 0],
            [0, 0, 0, 1, 0, 1, 0, 1, 1, 1, 1, 0, 1, 1, 0],
            [0, 1, 0, 1, 0, 1, 0, 0, 0, 0, 1, 0, 1, 0, 0],
            [0, 1, 0, 1, 0, 1, 1, 1, 1, 0, 1, 0, 1, 1, 0],
            [0, 1, 0, 1, 0, 0, 0, 0, 1, 0, 1, 0, 0, 0, 0],
            [0, 1, 0, 1, 1, 1, 1, 0, 1, 0, 1, 0, 1, 1, 0],
            [0, 1, 0, 0, 0, 0, 1, 0, 1, 0, 1, 0, 0, 1, 0],
            [0, 1, 1, 1, 1, 0, 1, 0, 1, 0, 1, 0, 1, 1, 0],
            [0, 0, 0, 0, 1, 0, 1, 0, 1, 0, 1, 0, 0, 0, 0],
            [0, 1, 1, 0, 1, 0, 1, 0, 1, 0, 1, 1, 1, 1, 0],
            [0, 0, 1, 0, 1, 0, 0, 0, 1, 0, 0, 0, 0, 1, 0],
            [0, 1, 1, 1, 1, 1, 1, 1, 1, 1, 1, 0, 1, 0],
            [0, 0, 0, 0, 0, 0, 0, 0, 0, 0, 0, 0, 0, 1, 0]
        ]
    ...
```

Listing 10-4: maze_solver.py

Next, we add the code to check whether we can move to a cell:

```python
def can_move(self, row, col):
    #Check if we can move to this cell
    return (0 <= row < self.ROWS \
            and 0 <= col < self.COLS \
            and self.matrix[row][col] == 0)
```

Listing 10-5: maze_solver.py

The cell must be within the maze bounds and should be part of a corridor.

We also provide a method to print the maze:

```python
def print_maze(self):
    #Print the maze
    for row in self.matrix:
        print(" ".join(str(cell) for cell in row))
```

Listing 10-6: maze_solver.py

The following method implements the maze solving algorithm:

```python
def solve(self, row, col):
    #Solve the maze using backtracking
    if row == self.ROWS - 1 and col == self.COLS - 1:
```

```python
            #Destination reached
            self.stack.push(Point(row, col))
            return 1

        if self.can_move(row, col):
            self.stack.push(Point(row, col))
            self.matrix[row][col] = 2   #Mark as visited

            #Move right
            if self.solve(row, col + 1) == 1:
                return 1

            #Move down
            if self.solve(row + 1, col) == 1:
                return 1

            #Move left
            if self.solve(row, col - 1) == 1:
                return 1

            #Move up
            if self.solve(row - 1, col) == 1:
                return 1

            #Backtrack if no movement is possible
            self.stack.pop()
            return 0

        return 0
```

Listing 10-7: maze_solver.py

First of all, we check whether the destination has been reached, by comparing the current row and column with the constant values ROWS and COLS.

In the opposite case, we first check if we can actually move to this cell, i.e., if it is part of a corridor and is within the maze bounds. If so, we add its coordinates into the stack and we mark the cell with the number 2, to mark the fact that we have already passed from this cell.

Then, we proceed with calling recursively the solve() method for all four directions, starting with right and down, and then trying with left and up. If none of those movements results in solving the maze (i.e. they all return 0), then we will have to backtrack. Since this point in the maze was not eventually part of the solution, we pop it from the stack.

We also define a method to print the path followed to solve the maze. We get it by popping the visited cells of the maze from the stack, one by one:

```python
def print_path(self):
    #Print the path from stack
    while not self.stack.is_empty():
        p = self.stack.pop()
```

```
        print(f"({p.row}, {p.col})", end=", ")
```
Listing 10-8: maze_solver.py

Finally, let's see the main function of the program:

```
def main():
    maze = Maze()

    print("This is the maze:")
    maze.print_maze()

    if maze.solve(0, 0) == 1:
        print("\n\nThis is the path found:")
        maze.print_path()

        print("\n\nThis is the maze with all the points crossed:")
        maze.print_maze()
    else:
        print("No path found")

if __name__ == "__main__":
    main()
```
Listing 10-9: maze_solver.py

We first print the initial maze, then we solve the maze. Next, we print the solution path. Finally, we display the map once more; all the points that we crossed during our search will be marked with '2'.

You can find this project in GitHub:

https://github.com/htset/python_exercises_dsa/tree/master/MazeSolver

11. File Indexer

For this exercise, we will create a program that will recursively index all the files in a specified folder. The information about the indexed files (filename and location in the disk) will be stored in a *Binary Search Tree (BST)* for faster searching.

Proposed Solution

The Binary Search Tree structure is a tree where each node has only two children, left and right. Here is the definition of the class:

```python
import os

class FileIndexer:
    class Node:
        def __init__(self, name, path):
            self.fileName = name
            self.filePath = path
            self.left = None
            self.right = None

    def __init__(self):
        self.root = None

    ...
```

Listing 11-1: file_indexer.py

Each node of the tree contains two strings, the file name and the file location. It also contains references to the two children nodes.

Next, we define a method to insert a new node into the tree:

```python
    def insert_node(self, file_name, file_path):
        #Insert node into the tree
        if self.root is None:
            self.root = self.Node(file_name, file_path)
            return

        current = self.root
        while True:
            if file_name < current.fileName:
                if current.left is None:
                    current.left = self.Node(file_name, file_path)
                    return
                current = current.left
            else:
                if current.right is None:
                    current.right = self.Node(file_name, file_path)
                    return
                current = current.right
```

Listing 11-2: file_indexer.py

Starting from the root of the tree, we move downwards to the left or to the right depending on the inserted value.

Next, we define the method that will recursively index all files into the tree:

```python
def index_directory_helper(self, dir_path):
    #If it's not a directory, return
    if not os.path.isdir(dir_path):
        return

    #Loop over files within the directory
    with os.scandir(dir_path) as entries:
        for entry in entries:
            if entry.is_file():
                self.insert_node(entry.name, entry.path)

    #Loop over directories within the directory
    with os.scandir(dir_path) as entries:
        for entry in entries:
            if entry.is_dir():
                #Recursive indexing
                self.index_directory_helper(entry.path)
```

Listing 11-3: file_indexer.py

We first check if a path exists and corresponds to a directory (`os.path.isdir`). We then loop over all the files inside the directory, one by one, and we insert them in the tree as new nodes.

Then, we loop over the directories and also index them recursively.

Next, we define a method to recursively delete the nodes of the tree:

```python
def delete_subtree(self, root):
    if root is not None:
        self.delete_subtree(root.left)
        self.delete_subtree(root.right)
        root = None
```

Listing 11-4: file_indexer.py

We perform this by setting the root of the subtree to null, so that the subtree will be removed by the garbage collector.

Then, we have the directory traversal method (also recursive):

```python
def traverse(self, root):
    if root is not None:
        self.traverse(root.left)
        print(f"{root.fileName}: {root.filePath}")
        self.traverse(root.right)
```

Listing 11-5: file_indexer.py

Now, we define methods to index and print all the files in a directory. Those methods call the respective helper methods:

```python
def index_directory(self, directory_path):
    self.root = None
    self.index_directory_helper(directory_path)

def print_files(self):
    print("Indexed files:")
    self.traverse(self.root)
```

Listing 11-6: file_indexer.py

After the tree has been set up, we can call method search_file_location() to get the location of a file:

```python
def search_file_location(self, filename):
    #Search for a file in the BST
    current = self.root
    while current is not None:
        if filename == current.fileName:
            return current.filePath   #File found
        elif filename < current.fileName:
            current = current.left    #Search in the left subtree
        else:
            current = current.right   #Search in the right subtree
    return ""   #File not found
```

Listing 11-7: file_indexer.py

We traverse the tree until we find a node with the specified file name. If the tree is exhausted, then we return an empty string.

Finally, here is the main code:

```python
if __name__ == "__main__":
    path = input("Path to index recursively: ")

    indexer = FileIndexer()
    indexer.index_directory(path)
    indexer.print_files()

    filename_to_search = input("Let's search for a file's location. "
                               "Give the file name: ")

    location = indexer.search_file_location(filename_to_search)
    if location:
        print(f"File {filename_to_search} found. Location: {location}")
    else:
        print(f"File {filename_to_search} not found.")
```

Listing 11-8: file_indexer.py

Users can index the contents of a folder and then they can search for a specific filename.

You can find this project in GitHub:

https://github.com/htset/python_exercises_dsa/tree/master/FileIndexer

12. Inventory with AVL Tree

In this exercise, we will create an inventory program, that will store information about the company's products in an AVL tree structure.

Proposed Solution

An *AVL (Adelson-Velsky and Landis) tree* is a *self-balancing* binary search tree structure. With the term *balanced*, we mean that both branches of the tree have the same depth or differ by one level at the most. To achieve this, a process called *rebalancing* is occasionally performed, that changes the tree structure in way that the tree is closer to be balanced.

The AVL tree has almost the same structure as a simple binary search tree (BST); the difference lies in the rebalancing algorithm. Let's see the structure:

```python
import random

class Product:
    def __init__(self, id, name, price, quantity):
        self.id = id
        self.name = name
        self.price = price
        self.quantity = quantity

class InventoryNode:
    def __init__(self, product):
        self.product = product
        self.left = None
        self.right = None
        self.height = 1
```

Listing 12-1: inventory.py

The `InventoryNode` class contains a product object and two references to the tree's branches. Most importantly, it also contains the `height` property, which is used to track the tree's height.

Next, we define the `Inventory` class, which contains a reference that is the root of the AVL tree. We also define two internal methods of the tree:

```python
class Inventory:
    def __init__(self):
        self.root = None

    def get_height(self, node):
        if node is None:
            return 0
        else:
            return node.height

    def get_balance(self, node):
        if node is None:
```

```
            return 0
        else:
            return self.get_height(node.left) - self.get_height(node.right)
```
Listing 12-2: inventory.py

The former gives us the height of the tree, while the latter checks whether the tree is balanced or not.

Afterwards, we add code for the creation of a new node in the tree:

```
    #Create a new node with the given product
    def new_node(self, product):
        return InventoryNode(product)
```
Listing 12-3: inventory.py

Note that the height of the node is set to 1 by the constructor.

Next, we proceed with the definition of two methods for the rotation of the tree to the left or to the right:

```
    #Right rotate subtree
    def rotate_right(self, y):
        x = y.left
        T2 = x.right

        #Perform rotation
        x.right = y
        y.left = T2

        #Update heights
        y.height = max(self.get_height(y.left), self.get_height(y.right)) + 1
        x.height = max(self.get_height(x.left), self.get_height(x.right)) + 1

        #Return new root
        return x

    #Left rotate subtree
    def rotate_left(self, x):
        y = x.right
        T2 = y.left

        #Perform rotation
        y.left = x
        x.right = T2

        #Update heights
        x.height = max(self.get_height(x.left), self.get_height(x.right)) + 1
        y.height = max(self.get_height(y.left), self.get_height(y.right)) + 1

        #Return new root
        return y
```
Listing 12-4: inventory.py

Those two methods will be used when we will try to insert a new node into the tree:

```python
#Insert a product in the AVL tree
def insert_product(self, node, product):
    if node is None:
        return self.new_node(product)

    #Insert the product
    if product.id < node.product.id:
        node.left = self.insert_product(node.left, product)
    elif product.id > node.product.id:
        node.right = self.insert_product(node.right, product)
    else:
        return node   #Duplicate IDs not allowed

    #Update height of this node
    node.height = 1 + max(self.get_height(node.left), \
                    self.get_height(node.right))

    #Get balance factor
    balance = self.get_balance(node)

    #Left Left Case
    if balance > 1 and product.id < node.left.product.id:
        return self.rotate_right(node)

    #Right Right Case
    if balance < -1 and product.id > node.right.product.id:
        return self.rotate_left(node)

    #Left Right Case
    if balance > 1 and product.id > node.left.product.id:
        node.left = self.rotate_left(node.left)
        return self.rotate_right(node)

    #Right Left Case
    if balance < -1 and product.id < node.right.product.id:
        node.right = self.rotate_right(node.right)
        return self.rotate_left(node)

    return node
```

Listing 12-5: inventory.py

The idea here is to check for the tree balance after inserting a new node to it. If the tree becomes unbalanced, then we will have to rotate it either to the left or to the right.

Next, we present the methods to traverse the tree while printing its contents, as well as the code to search for a specific product in the tree:

```python
def traverse_tree(self, node):
    if node is not None:
        self.traverse_tree(node.left)
        print(f"ID: {node.product.id}, Name: {node.product.name}, "
```

```
            "Price: {node.product.price}, "
            "Quantity: {node.product.quantity}")
        self.traverse_tree(node.right)

def search_product(self, node, id):
    if node is None or node.product.id == id:
        if node is None:
            print("Product not found.")
        else:
            print(f"Found product: ID: {node.product.id}, "
                  "Name: {node.product.name}, "
                  "Price: {node.product.price}, "
                  "Quantity: {node.product.quantity}")
        return node

    print(f"Visited product ID: {node.product.id}")

    if id < node.product.id:
        return self.search_product(node.left, id)
    else:
        return self.search_product(node.right, id)
```

Listing 12-6: inventory.py

Traversing the tree means visiting each node in the tree, and this is performed recursively, first for the left branch and then for the right branch.

Searching for a product in the tree works in similar fashion: we visit a node, and we check the product's ID. If it matches the search ID, then we print the product details, and the method returns. Otherwise, we visit the left or the right branch of the tree recursively, depending on the search ID.

All the methods we have defined so far are not to be used directly. We define three methods that will call them:

```
def insert_product_public(self, product):
    self.root = self.insert_product(self.root, product)

def traverse_tree_public(self):
    self.traverse_tree(self.root)

def search_product_public(self, id):
    return self.search_product(self.root, id)
```

Listing 12-7: inventory.py

We use this convention because the respective methods (insert_product, traverse_tree and search_product) are called recursively. In this way, we provide a clean interface to programmers that will use our code.

Finally, here is the main code:

```
if __name__ == "__main__":
```

```python
inv = Inventory()
products = []

#Initialize products with random values
for i in range(100):
    products.append(Product(id=i + 1, \
                        name=f"Product {i + 1}", \
                        price=random.uniform(0, 100), \
                        quantity=random.randint(1, 100)))

#Shuffle products list
random.shuffle(products)

#Insert products into the inventory
for product in products:
    inv.insert_product_public(product)

#Display all products in the inventory
print("Inventory:")
inv.traverse_tree_public()

#Search for a specific product
product_id_to_search = 35
found_product = inv.search_product_public(product_id_to_search)
if found_product is not None:
    print(f"Product found: ID: {found_product.product.id}, "
          "Name: {found_product.product.name}, "
          "Price: {found_product.product.price}, "
          "Quantity: {found_product.product.quantity}")
else:
    print(f"Product with ID {product_id_to_search} not found.")
```

Listing 12-8: inventory.py

We create 100 products with random quantities and prices and place them in a list. Then we shuffle the list in a random order. Afterwards, we insert the products into the AVL tree, and we print its contents.

Finally, a search is performed for a specific product ID. During the search process we print the visited nodes to get an idea of how fast we will find the specific ID inside the AVL tree.

You can find this project in GitHub:

https://github.com/htset/python_exercises_dsa/tree/master/Inventory

13. Social Network

A social network is essentially a *graph* of nodes that depicts the users of the network along with their connections to their friends. In this exercise, we will create such a graph and we will implement the functionality to recommend new friends according to a user's current connections.

Proposed Solution

There are various ways to implement the users' graph, for example using *sparse two-dimensional matrices*. Here we will construct the graph with the use of a list of users, where the connections are stored in a linked list:

```python
class FriendNode:
    def __init__(self, name):
        self.name = name
        self.next = None

class User:
    def __init__(self, name):
        self.name = name
        self.friends = None
```

Listing 13-1: social_network.py

The User class contains the name of the user as well as a linked list of the user's friends.

Next, we define a *queue* class that will be used by the friend recommendation algorithm. For learning purposes, we will make our own queue instead of using the one from Python:

```python
class MyQueue:
    class QueueNode:
        def __init__(self, user_index):
            self.user_index = user_index
            self.next = None

    def __init__(self):
        self.front = self.rear = None

    def is_empty(self):
        return self.front is None

    def enqueue(self, user_index):
        new_node = self.QueueNode(user_index)
        if self.is_empty():
            self.front = self.rear = new_node
        else:
            self.rear.next = new_node
            self.rear = new_node

    def dequeue(self):
        if self.is_empty():
            print("Queue is empty!")
```

```
            return -1

    user_index = self.front.user_index
    self.front = self.front.next

    if self.front is None:
        self.rear = None

    return user_index
```
Listing 13-2: social_network.py

The queue contains the indexes of the users, as they will appear inside the users' list (see below in the Graph class). We define the class for the queue nodes, and methods to enqueue and dequeue user indexes inside the queue, as well as to check whether it is empty or not.

Now, let's see how we will insert users into the graph and how we will define the connections with their friends. We define the Graph class, that essentially contains a list of all the users of the social network:

```
class Graph:
    MAX_USERS = 100

    def __init__(self):
        self.users = [None] * self.MAX_USERS
        self.num_users = 0

    ...
```
Listing 13-3: social_network.py

Next, we provide the functionality to add a new user to the graph:

```
    def add_user(self, name):
        if self.num_users >= self.MAX_USERS:
            print("Max user limit reached!")
            return

        self.users[self.num_users] = User(name)
        self.num_users += 1
```
Listing 13-4: social_network.py

We use the following method to add a new connection to a user:

```
    def add_connection(self, src, dest):
        if src < 0 or src >= self.num_users \
            or dest < 0 or dest >= self.num_users:
            print("Invalid user index!")
            return

        #Add bidirectional connection
        new_friend_src = FriendNode(self.users[dest].name)
        new_friend_src.next = self.users[src].friends
```

```
        self.users[src].friends = new_friend_src

        new_friend_dest = FriendNode(self.users[src].name)
        new_friend_dest.next = self.users[dest].friends
        self.users[dest].friends = new_friend_dest
```

Listing 13-5: social_network.py

Note that when we add a new connection, we make it bidirectional. That is, we insert a friend node for each one of the connection's ends.

Next, we proceed to the more interesting stuff, the recommender method:

```
    def recommend_friends(self, user_index):
        print(f"Recommended friends for {self.users[user_index].name}:")

        #Store the indexes of the user's friends
        queue = MyQueue()
        #Store the persons that we have already visited
        visited = [False] * self.MAX_USERS

        visited[user_index] = True
        #Enqueue the starting user
        queue.enqueue(user_index)

        while not queue.is_empty():
            current_user_index = queue.dequeue()
            current = self.users[current_user_index].friends

            #Traverse the user's friends
            while current is not None:
                friend_index = -1
                #Find the friend's index
                for i in range(self.num_users):
                    if current.name == self.users[i].name:
                        friend_index = i
                        break

                #Check if the friend is already visited
                if friend_index != -1 and not visited[friend_index]:
                    print(f"- {current.name}")
                    #Add friend to visited list
                    visited[friend_index] = True
                    #Enqueue friend
                    queue.enqueue(friend_index)

                #Move to the next friend
                current = current.next
```

Listing 13-6: social_network.py

The `recommend_friends()` method uses *breadth-first search (BFS)* to traverse the social network graph, starting from the specified user and visiting all connected users to recommend friends. It marks users as visited (using the `visited` list) to avoid recommending the same friend multiple times and enqueues each friend to ensure all potential friends are discovered and recommended.

The BFS algorithm makes use of a queue, where we store the indexes of the user's friends as we follow the linked list. We then use the queue to get the friends of the user's friends, and in this way, we are able to travel through the connections of the graph and find all the connected people to the specific user.

Finally, here is the main code:

```python
if __name__ == "__main__":
    graph = Graph()
    graph.add_user("User A")
    graph.add_user("User B")
    graph.add_user("User C")
    graph.add_user("User D")
    graph.add_user("User E")
    graph.add_user("User F")
    graph.add_user("User G")
    graph.add_user("User H")

    graph.add_connection(0, 1)
    graph.add_connection(1, 2)
    graph.add_connection(2, 3)
    graph.add_connection(4, 5)
    graph.add_connection(5, 7)
    graph.add_connection(3, 6)

    graph.recommend_friends(0)
    graph.recommend_friends(1)
    graph.recommend_friends(7)
```

Listing 13-7: social_network.py

Here, we add users to the graph, and we enter their friend connections. Then we run the algorithm to get friend recommendations.

You can find this project in GitHub:

https://github.com/htset/python_exercises_dsa/tree/master/SocialNetwork

14. Flights

Let's create a console application that will maintain a list of flights between cities and that will find the best combination of flights in terms of ticket cost.

Proposed Solution

This problem involves creating a graph between the cities. This graph will be weighted, with the cost of the respective ticket. We will use *Dijkstra's algorithm* to find the cheapest path between two of those cities.

First, we define the `City` class that will store a dictionary of the connected cities and the respective costs:

```
import heapq

class City:
    def __init__(self, name):
        self.name = name
        self.flights = {}
```

Listing 14-1: flights.py

Next, we define the `FlightGraph` class:

```
class FlightGraph:
    def __init__(self):
        self.cities = {}

    ...
```

Listing 14-2: flights.py

This class contains all the cities objects in a map along with their names. We can add cities and flights to our graph with the following methods:

```
    #Add a city to the graph
    def add_city(self, name):
        self.cities[name] = City(name)

    #Add a flight between two cities and its cost
    def add_flight(self, src, dest, cost):
        #Assuming flights are bidirectional
        self.cities[src].flights[dest] = cost
        self.cities[dest].flights[src] = cost
```

Listing 14-3: flights.py

Note that we assume that flights are bidirectional, and that they have the same price in both directions.

Next, we calculate the cheapest route between two cities using Dijkstra's algorithm:

```python
#Function to find the cheapest route between two cities
# using Dijkstra's algorithm
def find_cheapest_route(self, src, dest):
    dist = {city: float('inf') for city in self.cities}
    prev = {city: None for city in self.cities}
    pq = []

    dist[src] = 0
    heapq.heappush(pq, (0, src))

    while pq:
        u_dist, u = heapq.heappop(pq)

        #Process each neighbor of the current node
        for v, cost in self.cities[u].flights.items():
            if dist[u] != float('inf') and dist[u] + cost < dist[v]:
                dist[v] = dist[u] + cost
                prev[v] = u
                heapq.heappush(pq, (dist[v], v))

    #Reconstructing the path from source to destination
    path = []
    at = dest
    while at is not None:
        path.append(at)
        at = prev[at]
    path.reverse()

    return path, dist[dest]
```

Listing 14-4: flights.py

Initially, we initialize a dictionary to store the distances from the source city to every other city, marking the source city's distance as 0 and all other cities as *infinity*. We use a priority queue to process cities based on their distance from the source, dequeuing the city with the shortest distance first.

For each dequeued city, we examine its neighboring cities, updating their distances if a shorter path through the current city is found. This process continues until all cities are visited or until the destination city is reached.

Upon completion, we reconstruct the shortest path from the source to the destination using the information stored in the previous node map, facilitating the determination of the total price of the route.

To avoid getting stuck in loops during the graph traversal, we keep track of the cities visited in the current path (`dist` map). If a city has already been visited in the current path, we skip exploring flights from that city to prevent loops.

We can calculate and print all the possible flights between two cities using *Depth-First Search (DFS)*:

```python
    #Display all possible flights between two cities using DFS
    def display_all_flights(self, src, dest):
        if src not in self.cities or dest not in self.cities:
            print("Invalid cities entered.")
            return

        visited = set()
        path = [src]
        self.dfs(src, dest, visited, path)
```
Listing 14-5: flights.py

We see that method display_all_flights() calls the recursive dfs() method:

```python
    #Recursive DFS function to find all flights
    # between source and destination
    def dfs(self, src, dest, visited, path):
        visited.add(src)

        if src == dest:
            self.print_path(path)
        else:
            for flight in self.cities[src].flights:
                if flight not in visited:
                    path.append(flight)
                    self.dfs(flight, dest, visited, path)
                    path.pop()

        visited.remove(src)
```
Listing 14-6: flights.py

The dfs() method in the FlightGraph class implements *Depth-First Search (DFS)* recursively to find all possible flights between a source and a destination city within a flight network.

It begins by marking the current city as visited and checks if it matches the destination city. If the destination is reached, it prints the current path. Otherwise, it explores all neighboring cities not yet visited by recursively calling itself for each neighbor.

During exploration, it pushes the neighboring city onto the path stack and continues the search until all possible paths from the current city are explored or until the destination is reached.

Upon backtracking, it removes the current city from the path stack and marks it as unvisited, allowing exploration of alternative paths. This process is repeated until all cities in the network are explored.

We use the aforementioned stack to print the final path in print_path() method:

```python
    #Helper function to print a path (list content)
    def print_path(self, path):
        print(" -> ".join(path))  }
```
Listing 14-7: flights.py

Finally in the main code, we add cities and flights to the graph, and we ask the user to select a pair of cities to calculate the best (cheapest) combination of flights:

```python
if __name__ == "__main__":
    graph = FlightGraph()

    graph.add_city("London")
    graph.add_city("Paris")
    graph.add_city("Berlin")
    graph.add_city("Rome")
    graph.add_city("Madrid")
    graph.add_city("Amsterdam")

    graph.add_flight("London", "Paris", 100)
    graph.add_flight("London", "Berlin", 150)
    graph.add_flight("London", "Madrid", 200)
    graph.add_flight("Paris", "Berlin", 120)
    graph.add_flight("Paris", "Rome", 180)
    graph.add_flight("Berlin", "Rome", 220)
    graph.add_flight("Madrid", "Rome", 250)
    graph.add_flight("Madrid", "Amsterdam", 170)
    graph.add_flight("Amsterdam", "Berlin", 130)

    departure = input("Enter departure city: ")
    destination = input("Enter destination city: ")

    #Display all possible flights
    print(f"All possible flights between {departure} and {destination}:")
    graph.display_all_flights(departure, destination)

    #Find the cheapest route and total price
    route, total_price = graph.find_cheapest_route(departure, destination)

    #Display the cheapest route and total price
    print("Cheapest Route: " + " -> ".join(route))
    print("Total Price: " + str(total_price))
```

Listing 14-8: flights.py

You can find this project in GitHub:

https://github.com/htset/python_exercises_dsa/tree/master/Flights

15. MNIST Image Comparison

In this exercise, we will play with handwriting images from the MNIST database.

Proposed Solution

The MNIST database (http://yann.lecun.com/exdb/mnist/) is a set of images depicting handwritten digits. The images are of 28x28 dimension and are typically used when studying pattern recognition and machine learning techniques.

Source: Wikipedia

We will download the following file and we will unzip it in our project's directory:

http://yann.lecun.com/exdb/mnist/train-images-idx3-ubyte.gz

We will also rename it as *input.dat*.

The first 15 bytes of this file, contain metadata about the images, i.e. the number of the images and their dimensions. Therefore, we will start reading from the 16th byte in steps of 28x28=784 bytes.

First, we define the `Image` class that will store the image data in a list of bytes:

```
import random
import math

class Image:
    def __init__(self, data, id):
```

```python
        self.data = data[:]
        self.id = id

    def print_image(self):
        for i in range(len(self.data)):
            if self.data[i] == 0:
                print(" ", end="")
            else:
                print("*", end="")
            if (i + 1) % 28 == 0:
                print()

    def euclidean_distance(self, img):
        distance = 0.0
        for i in range(len(self.data)):
            distance += (self.data[i] - img.data[i]) ** 2
        return math.sqrt(distance)
```

Listing 15-1: MNIST_images.py

Inside the class, we implement the Image constructor and a method that prints the image as a series of asterisks.

We also implement the method that will calculate the *Euclidean distance* between two images, the current image and another one passed as method parameter. We are essentially calculating the sum of the differences between the respective bytes of two images. If the images are similar in content, then the distance will be minimized. Conversely, the distance will be higher, for images that have significant differences.

Now, let's see the main code:

```python
if __name__ == "__main__":
    images = []

    try:
        with open("input.dat", "rb") as file:
            #Skip the metadata at the beginning of the file
            file.seek(16)

            count = 0
            while True:
                pixels = file.read(784)
                if len(pixels) == 0:
                    break
                images.append(Image(list(pixels), count))
                count += 1

    except IOError as e:
        print(e)

    print("Total images:", len(images))

    #Example: Find the closest image to a randomly selected image
```

```python
#Seed the random number generator
rand = random.Random()

#Generate a random index within the range of the list length
random_index = rand.randint(0, len(images) - 1)
print("Random index:", random_index)

random_image = images[random_index]
random_image.print_image()

closest_image = None
min_distance = float('inf')
min_index = 0

for i in range(len(images)):
    distance = random_image.euclidean_distance(images[i])
    if distance != 0 and distance < min_distance:
        min_distance = distance
        min_index = i
        closest_image = images[i]

#Output the label of the closest image
print("\nClosest image (distance={}, "
      "index={})\n".format(min_distance, min_index))

#Print closest image
if closest_image:
    closest_image.print_image()
```

Listing 15-2: MNIST_images.py

We use a list to store the image references. After we open the *input.dat* binary file, we skip the first 15 bytes with `seek()`. Then, in a loop, we read one image at a time (784 bytes) with `read()` into a buffer and we copy them to the respective `Image` object into the list.

Afterwards, we get a randomly selected image from the list, and we print it using empty space where the byte is zero and an asterisk ('*') in places where the image bytes are non-zero. This way, we can get an idea of the handwriting digit that was chosen:

```
Total images: 60000
Random index: 24224


                    ****
                    *****
                    ******
                    ****
                   ****
                   ****
                  ****
                  *****
                  ****
                 ****
                 *******
                 *********
                 **********
                 ****   ***
                 ***    ***
                 ***    ***
                 ***  *****
                 ********
                 *******
                 ******
```

After printing the selected image, we iterate the images list, and we calculate the Euclidian distance between the randomly selected image and the currently selected image from the list. We maintain the minimum distance encountered and the corresponding image along with its ID.

At the end, we print the closest image that we got; it seems that the algorithm is working fine.

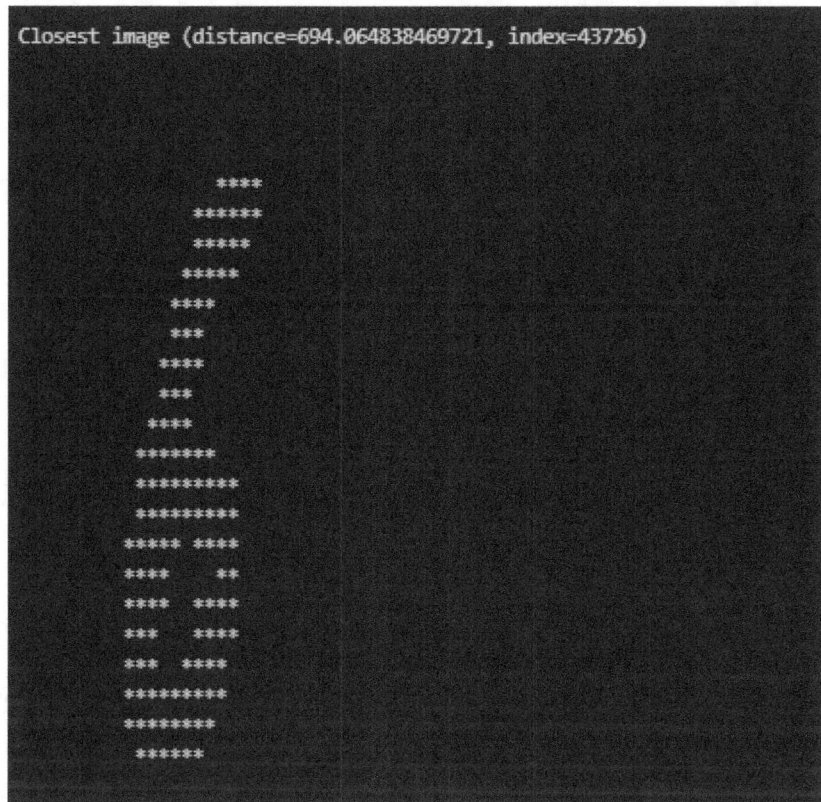

As a final note, this algorithm will take a lot of time to get the closest image, as it is checking all the images, one by one. There are other algorithms that will make this operation faster, albeit, with a loss of precision.

One such example is the Locality-Sensitive Hashing[2] (LSH) algorithm, a technique used for approximate nearest neighbor search in high-dimensional spaces. LSH is particularly useful when dealing with large datasets where traditional exact nearest neighbor search methods become computationally expensive.

You can find this project in GitHub:

https://github.com/htset/python_exercises_dsa/tree/master/MNISTImages

---

[2] https://en.wikipedia.org/wiki/Locality-sensitive_hashing

16. HTTP Server with Caching

In this exercise, we will create a simple HTTP server that will serve static content (only HTML files). The web server will make use of a cache mechanism that will keep the most recently served content, in order to boost the server's performance.

Proposed Solution

The web server cache is a structure that stores the content that was previously sent to the client browser. The cache has limited space, so when it is filled up, we will need to empty the *least recently used (LRU)* entry in order to make space for the new entry. Moreover, when an entry is used by the server to send content to the client, then this entry is moved to the head of the list, as it is the more recently used entry.

Let's see the cache definition:

```
import socket

class LRUCache:
    CACHE_SIZE = 3

    class Node:
        def __init__(self, url, content):
            self.url = url
            self.content = content
            self.prev = None
            self.next = None

    def __init__(self):
        #Initialize the cache
        self.head = None
        self.tail = None
        self.size = 0

...
```
Listing 16-1: web_server_cache.py

The cache is implemented as a *doubly linked list*. In this kind of linked list, we can move to both directions, forward and backward. The doubly linked list is beneficial in our case as we can efficiently remove and insert nodes anywhere in the list without needing to traverse the list from the beginning. The same effect could be achieved with simple linked lists, or even arrays, but with lower performance.

Let's skip the rest of the cache definition for now, and jump to the main() method of our program:

```
def main():
    #Start the HTTP server
    server = HttpServer()
    server.start()
```

```python
if __name__ == "__main__":
    main()
```

Listing 16-2: web_server_cache.py

Here, we create an object of the `HttpServer` class, that will handle the connections with the clients. Let's see how it is implemented:

```python
class HttpServer:
    PORT = 8080
    MAX_REQUEST_SIZE = 1024

    def __init__(self):
        self.cache = LRUCache()

    def start(self):
        #Start the HTTP server
        with socket.socket(socket.AF_INET, socket.SOCK_STREAM) as server:
            server.bind(('localhost', self.PORT))
            server.listen()
            print("Server started on port", self.PORT)
            while True:
                client, _ = server.accept()
                self.handle_request(client)
                client.close()

    def handle_request(self, client):
        #Handle incoming HTTP requests
        with client:
            request = client.recv(self.MAX_REQUEST_SIZE).decode('utf-8')
            print("Received request:", request)

            parts = request.split()
            if len(parts) < 2 or parts[0] != "GET":
                print("Invalid request format.")
                return

            url = parts[1]
            content = self.cache.get_content(url)

            if not content:
                try:
                    with open(url[1:], 'r', encoding='utf-8') as file:
                        content = file.read()
                        print("Got content from file:", content)
                        self.cache.put_content(url, content)
                except FileNotFoundError:
                    print("File not found:", url[1:])
                    content = "HTTP/1.1 404 Not Found\r\n\r\n"
                except IOError:
                    print("File not found:", url[1:])
                    content = "HTTP/1.1 404 Not Found\r\n\r\n"
            else:
```

```
            print("Serving content from cache.")

        content_type = "text/plain"
        if url.endswith((".html", ".htm")):
            content_type = "text/html"

        response = f"HTTP/1.1 200 OK\r\n"
                   "Content-Type: {content_type}\r\n\r\n{content}"

        client.sendall(response.encode('utf-8'))
```
Listing 16-3: web_server_cache.py

Here we create a server socket that continuously accepts HTTP connections from web browsers at port 8080. When a connection is accepted, then the `handle_request()` method is called.

Initially, the web request string is split in order to retrieve the request type and the URL; only GET requests are handled by our server.

We then use the request URL to search in the cache for a previously stored response for this URL. If such an entry is not found in the cache, then we open the requested HTML file (The HTML files are stored in the same folder as our script), and we transmit its HTML content in the response. Note that, before sending the content, we must send the header of the response:

`HTTP/1.1 200 OK\nContent-Type: text/html`

If the URL is found in the cache, then we get the content from there and we send it with the response.

Let's see how we do this, in method `get_content()` from the `LRUCache` class:

```
    def get_content(self, url):
        #Get content associated with a URL from the cache
        current = self.head
        while current:
            if current.url == url:
                #Move the accessed node to the head
                self.move_to_head(current)
                print("Got content from cache:", current.content)
                return current.content
            current = current.next
        return ""
```
Listing 16-4: web_server_cache.py

We start from the head of the list, and we search for the URL in the cache's nodes. If we find the URL, then we move the node to the head of the cache (the *most recently used entry*) and we return the stored HTML content. The method returns an empty string if the URL is not found in the cache.

When a page is read from its file, then we store its content into the cache, with put_content():

```python
def put_content(self, url, content):
    #Put a URL-content pair into the cache
    if self.size == self.CACHE_SIZE:
        #If cache is full, remove the least recently used node
        self.delete_node(self.tail)
        self.size -= 1
    new_node = self.create_node(url, content)
    self.insert_at_head(new_node)
    self.size += 1
```

Listing 16-5: web_server_cache.py

If we have reached the maximum cache size, then the *LRU algorithm* kicks in: we delete the least recently used entry (the node at the tail of the list) and we make space for the insertion of the new entry (at the head of the list).

Now we can examine the methods that handle the cache operations. First, let's see how we can create a new node:

```python
def create_node(self, url, content):
    #Create a new node
    print("New node created:", content)
    return self.Node(url, content)
```

Listing 16-6: web_server_cache.py

Next, we see how to insert a new node at the head of the cache:

```python
def insert_at_head(self, node):
    #Insert a new node at the head of the cache
    node.next = self.head
    node.prev = None
    if self.head:
        self.head.prev = node
    self.head = node
    if not self.tail:
        self.tail = node
    print("Node inserted at head:", node.content)
```

Listing 16-7: web_server_cache.py

Note that in all operations we have to take care of all four references: `head`, `tail`, `next`, `prev`.

As part of the LRU algorithm, we have to move a node to the head of the list:

```python
def move_to_head(self, node):
```

```
    #Move a node to the head of the cache
    if node == self.head:
        return
    if node.prev:
        node.prev.next = node.next
    if node.next:
        node.next.prev = node.prev
    node.prev = None
    node.next = self.head
    if self.head:
        self.head.prev = node
    self.head = node
    if not self.tail:
        self.tail = node
    print("Node moved to head:", node.content)
```

Listing 16-8: web_server_cache.py

Finally, here is the code for node deletion:

```
def delete_node(self, node):
    #Delete a node from the cache
    if not node:
        return
    if node == self.head:
        self.head = node.next
    if node == self.tail:
        self.tail = node.prev
    if node.prev:
        node.prev.next = node.next
    if node.next:
        node.next.prev = node.prev
    print("Node deleted:", node.content)
```

Listing 16-9: web_server_cache.py

You can find this project in GitHub:

https://github.com/htset/python_exercises_dsa/tree/master/WebServerCache

17. Distributed Auction

In this exercise, we will create a distributed auction, that will consist of an auction server that receives bids from multiple clients. The clients will communicate with the server via sockets. The server will wait for 20 seconds (using a timer) for a new bid, or else the auction is over and the maximum bid wins. The timer will be reset upon timely submission of new bid.

Proposed Solution

Let's start wih the auction server. The server should be able to accommodate multiple clients. For this reason, each client will be served in a separate *thread*, that will be spawned when the server socket accepts a new connection:

```
import socket
import threading
import time

#Client class representing each client connected to the server
class Client:
    def __init__(self, socket, client_id):
        self.socket = socket
        self.writer = socket.makefile('w')
        self.reader = socket.makefile('r')
        self.id = client_id

...
```
Listing 17-1: auction_server.py

Here we define the `Client` class that stores information about the connected client (its ID and the corresponding socket, writer and reader objects).

The writer is responsible for sending data from the server to the client. In Python, this is typically done using a file-like object created from the socket, which allows the server to write strings to the socket as if it were writing to a file. The same holds for the reader object, but this time for reading from the client.

Next, we have the definition of the server's global variables:

```
#Constants
PORT = 8080   #Port number for the server
MAX_CLIENTS = 5   #Maximum number of clients

#Server and clients
server = None
clients = [None] * MAX_CLIENTS   #List to hold clients

#Auction details
best_bid = 0   #Highest bid received
winning_client = 0   #Client ID of the highest bidder
```

```python
#Timer for auction end
timer_event = threading.Event()
```

Listing 17-2: auction_server.py

Now we present the `main()` method:

```python
#Main function to start the server
def main():
    global server, timer_event

    try:
        server = socket.socket(socket.AF_INET, socket.SOCK_STREAM)
        server.bind(('localhost', PORT))
        server.listen(5)

        print("Server started. Waiting for connections...")

        #Start the timer
        timer_thread = threading.Thread(target=timer_completion_routine,
                                        args=(20, timer_event))
        timer_thread.start()

        while not timer_event.is_set():
            try:
                #Accept a new client connection
                server.settimeout(1)
                client_socket, _ = server.accept()
                print("Client connected:", client_socket.getpeername())

                #Find an available slot for the client
                client_id = -1
                for i in range(MAX_CLIENTS):
                    if clients[i] is None:
                        client_id = i
                        clients[i] = Client(client_socket, client_id + 1)
                        print("Client no.", client_id + 1, "connected.")
                        break

                #Handle client in a separate thread
                threading.Thread(target=handle_client, args=(client_id,)).start()
            except socket.timeout:
                continue

    except Exception as ex:
        print("Server error:", ex)
    finally:
        if server:
            server.close()
```

Listing 17-3: auction_server.py

We open a new server socket, and we listen for new connections. We also start a timer with 20 seconds duration. When the timer expires, then the `timer_completion_routine()` method will be called, ending the auction process.

When a new connection arrives, we store the client details in the clients' list, and we spawn a new thread. The thread will run the `handle_client()` method, that will handle the communication with the specific client.

Now, let's see the `handle_client()` method:

```python
#Handle client bids
def handle_client(client_id):
    global best_bid, winning_client, timer_event

    try:
        client = clients[client_id]

        while not timer_event.is_set():
            bid = client.reader.readline().strip()
            if not bid:
                #Client disconnected
                print("Client disconnected:", client.socket.getpeername())
                clients[client_id] = None
                break

            bid_amount = int(bid)
            print("Received bid", bid_amount, "from client", client.id)

            if bid_amount > best_bid:
                best_bid = bid_amount
                winning_client = client.id

                msg = "New best bid: {} (Client: {})".format(best_bid,
                                                              winning_client)
                broadcast_message(msg)
                print(msg)

                #Reset the timer
                timer_event.set()
                timer_event = threading.Event()
                threading.Thread(target=timer_completion_routine,
                                 args=(20, timer_event)).start()
            else:
                msg = "Received lower bid. Best bid remains at: {}".format(best_bid)
                broadcast_message(msg)
                print(msg)

    except Exception as ex:
        print("Client error:", ex)
```

Listing 17-4: auction_server.py

This method takes care of the communication with the client. It gets as input the client's ID, that was passed in main().

Then, in a while loop, it blocks in the reader.readLine() method, waiting for input from the client. When a message arrives, the method is unblocked and continues to check the input. If the bid is null, then the client has disconnected.

If the client has actually sent a valid bid, we compare it with the current maximum bid and we update this value if we got a higher bid. We also proceed with informing all clients about the submitted bid. We also reset the timer to get a new 20 seconds' period.

Next, we define the broadcast_message() method, that sends messages to the clients:

```python
#Broadcast message to all clients
def broadcast_message(msg):
    for client in clients:
        if client:
            try:
                client.writer.write(msg + '\n')
                client.writer.flush()
            except Exception as ex:
                print("Send failed:", ex)
```

Listing 17-5: auction_server.py

When the timer eventually expires, the timer_completion_routine() method will be called:

```python
#Timer completion routine when auction ends
def timer_completion_routine(duration, event):
    global best_bid, winning_client

    time.sleep(duration)
    if not event.is_set():
        print("Auction finished. Winning bid:", best_bid
              , ", winner: client no.", winning_client)

        msg = "Auction finished. Winning bid: {}, " \
              "winner: client no. {}".format(best_bid, winning_client)
        try:
            broadcast_message(msg)
        except Exception as ex:
            print("Broadcast message error:", ex)

        #Exit the program
        print("Exiting program...")
        event.set()
        exit()

if __name__ == "__main__":
    main()
```

Listing 17-6: auction_server.py

After informing all clients about the winning bid, we exit the program. The client sockets will be closed by the respective clients when they receive the message of the auction completion.

Now for the auction client, we first implement the `main()` method:

```
import socket
import threading

#Constants
PORT = 8080   # Port number to connect to the server
SERVER_IP = "127.0.0.1"   # Server IP address

client = None
is_running = True
receive_thread = None

#Main function to start the client
def main():
    global client, receive_thread, is_running

    #Connect to the server
    try:
        client = socket.socket(socket.AF_INET, socket.SOCK_STREAM)
        client.connect((SERVER_IP, PORT))
        print("Connected to server.")
    except Exception as ex:
        print("Connect failed:", ex)
        return

    #Start receive handler thread
    receive_thread = threading.Thread(target=receive_handler)
    receive_thread.start()

    #Send bids until the user quits
    try:
        while is_running:
            bid = input("\nEnter your bid (or 'q' to quit): ")
            if bid.lower() == 'q':
                is_running = False
                client.close()
                receive_thread.join()   #Wait for the receive thread to finish
                break

            try:
                client.sendall((bid + '\n').encode('utf-8'))
            except Exception as ex:
                print("Send failed:", ex)
                return
    except Exception as e:
        print("Error:", e)
    finally:
        #Ensure client is closed
        if client:
```

```
            client.close()
```
Listing 17-7: auction_client.py

Here, we create a socket object, and we connect to the server. If the connection is successful, we spawn a new thread that will be used to receive and print the information from the server.

The sending part of the communication, i.e. the submission of bids to the server, will be performed by the main thread. If we had the same thread handle sending and receiving of data, we would have a problem, as the readLine() method would block and would not let the user send a new bid.

Here is the callback method for the thread handler:

```
#Handle incoming messages from the server
def receive_handler():
    global is_running
    try:
        while is_running:
            message = client.recv(1024).decode('utf-8')
            if not message:
                print("\nServer disconnected.")
                is_running = False
                break

            print("\nServer:", message)

            if message.startswith("Auction"):
                print("Auction ended. Exiting program.")
                is_running = False
                break
    except Exception as ex:
        if is_running:
            print("Receive failed:", ex)

if __name__ == "__main__":
    main()
```

Listing 17-8: auction_client.py

This thread receives messages from the auction server and prints them in the console. When the final message, starting with "Auction" arrives, then it closes down the resources and exits the program.

You can find this project in GitHub:

https://github.com/htset/python_exercises_dsa/tree/master/Auction

www.ingramcontent.com/pod-product-compliance
Lightning Source LLC
Chambersburg PA
CBHW082216220526
45470CB00010B/3184